Lancaster County
SIGNS OF FAITH
CHURCH SIGNS FROM CENTRAL PENNSYLVANIA

Lancaster County
SIGNS OF FAITH
CHURCH SIGNS FROM CENTRAL PENNSYLVANIA

COMPILED BY PETE BECKARY
PHOTOGRAPHY BY DR. ROBERT LEAHY

ExponentialPublications

Copyright ©2003 by Exponential Publications.
Exponential Publications, PO Box 300, Intercourse, PA 17534-0300
Email: churchsigns@frontiernet.net

INTRODUCTION

The book you are about to experience started soon after we relocated to Lancaster County and noticed that there were a great number of churches in the area. We also noticed that many were very creative in putting catchy phrases on the signs in front of their church house.

Before long we knew what churches had phrases and how frequently they were changed—some as often as weekly. This would even influence the route we took when driving somewhere.

Our entire family began taking note of these enlightening, challenging, thoughtful, serious, and funny sayings that quickly became the text for this book. These phrases have brought on reactions from laughter to feelings of regret to serious pondering and more.

THE QUOTES IN THIS COLLECTION ARE VERY DIVERSE: THEY LOOK BACK—THEY LOOK AHEAD; THEY CHALLENGE—THEY MAKE US LAUGH; SOME ARE ORIGINALS—SOME WE'VE HEARD BEFORE; SOME ARE NEW—SOME ARE OLD; SOME ARE SERIOUS—SOME ARE PUNNY; SOME ARE OBVIOUS—SOME WE MISS THE POINT.

BECAUSE THESE QUOTES WERE FOUND IN FRONT OF CHURCHES WE THOUGHT IT VERY FITTING TO TAKE EACH ONE AND MATCH IT UP WITH A SCRIPTURE VERSE. THIS SHOULD BE PRACTICED IN ALL ASPECTS OF LIFE—BRINGING EVERY THOUGHT, SITUATION, AND EXPERIENCE BACK TO THE WORD OF GOD. THIS ALLOWS US TO SEE LIFE FROM GOD'S PERSPECTIVE AND EXPERIENCE THE RICHNESS AND RELEVANCY OF THE BIBLE.

WE HOPE THAT YOU ENJOY READING THROUGH THESE PHRASES AS MUCH AS WE ENJOYED COLLECTING THEM. WE HOPE THAT YOU ARE AS BLESSED BY READING THE MATCHING SCRIPTURE REFERENCES AS WE WERE IN FINDING THEM IN THE BIBLE.

PEOPLE ARE

AT THE HEART

OF GOD'S HEART

*The preparations of the heart in man, and the answer of the tongue,
is from the LORD. — Proverbs 16:1*

24 HOUR LIFEGUARD ON DUTY

SEE JOHN 3:16

For God so loved the world, that he gave his only begotten Son,
that whosoever believeth in him should not perish, but have everlasting life. — John 3:16

GOD'S PROMISES

ARE GUARANTEED

FOR ETERNITY

And I give unto them eternal life; and they shall never perish, neither shall any man pluck them out of my hand. —John 10:28

ONLY GOD'S LOVE
WILL CHANGE OUR WORLD

I am come that they might have life,
and that they might have it more abundantly. —*John 10:10*

SLOW DOWN

AND LET GOD LOVE YOU

LIKE NEVER BEFORE

And the Lord direct your hearts into the love of God,
and into the patient waiting for Christ. —2 Thessalonians 3:5

GOD'S LOVE

TOUGH AND TENDER

Hereby perceive we the love of God, because he laid down his life for us: and we ought to lay down our lives for the brethren. —1 John 3:16

WHOEVER BELIEVES IN THE SON

HAS ETERNAL LIFE

*And they said, Believe on the Lord Jesus Christ,
and thou shalt be saved, and thy house. —Acts 16:31*

FREE TRIP TO HEAVEN

DETAILS INSIDE

Whosoever therefore shall confess me before men, him will I confess also before my Father which is in heaven. —Matthew 10:32-33

GOD HAS NO PROBLEMS

JUST PLANS

For I know the thoughts that I think toward you, saith the LORD, thoughts of peace, and not of evil, to give you an expected end. —*Jeremiah 29:11*

GOD'S RIGHTEOUSNESS

IS AVAILABLE FREE

TO ANYONE WHO ASKS HIM

And I say unto you, Ask, and it shall be given you; seek, and ye shall find; knock, and it shall be opened unto you. For every one that asketh receiveth; and he that seeketh findeth; and to him that knocketh it shall be opened —Luke 11:9-10

GOD CARES ABOUT YOU

Humble yourselves therefore under the mighty hand of God, that he may exalt you in due time: Casting all your care upon him; for he careth for you. —1 Peter 5:6-7

GOD'S LOVE FOR YOU IS REAL

*Verily, verily, I say unto you, He that heareth my word,
and believeth on him that sent me, hath everlasting life, and
shall not come into condemnation; but is passed from death unto life.* —John 5:24

ULTIMATE REALITY:

GOD IS

GOD LOVES

GOD CAN BE FOUND

*And ye shall seek me, and find me,
when ye shall search for me with all your heart.* —Jeremiah 29:13

GOD'S GRACE —

NOTHING WILL MAKE GOD

LOVE US MORE OR LOVE US LESS

For by grace are ye saved through faith; and that not of yourselves: it is the gift of God: Not of works, lest any man should boast. —Ephesians 2:8-9

FORBIDDEN FRUIT

CREATES MANY JAMS

But of the fruit of the tree which is in the midst of the garden, God hath said, Ye shall not eat of it, neither shall ye touch it, lest ye die. —Genesis 3:3

WILL THE ROAD YOU ARE ON

GET YOU TO MY PLACE?

*Because strait is the gate, and narrow is the way,
which leadeth unto life, and few there be that find it. —Matthew 7:14*

SIN WILL ALWAYS TAKE YOU

FARTHER THAN YOU WANT TO GO

Can a man take fire in his bosom, and his clothes not be burned?
Can one go upon hot coals, and his feet not be burned? — *Proverbs 6:27-28*

SIN WILL ALWAYS KEEP YOU LONGER

THAN YOU WANT TO STAY

None that go unto her return again, neither take they hold of the paths of life. — *Proverbs 2:17-19*

IT IS UNLIKELY THERE'LL BE A REDUCTION

IN THE WAGES OF SIN

*But now being made free from sin, and become servants to God, ye have your fruit
unto holiness, and the end everlasting life. For the wages of sin is death;
but the gift of God is eternal life through Jesus Christ our Lord.* —Romans 6:22-23

WILL YOUR ETERNAL HOME BE SMOKING OR NON-SMOKING?

And whosoever was not found written in the book of life was cast into the lake of fire. —Revelation 20:15

THE SIN WE TRY TO COVER UP

WILL EVENTUALLY BRING US DOWN

But if ye will not do so, behold, ye have sinned against the LORD: and be sure your sin will find you out. — Numbers 32:23

WE CAN ONLY APPRECIATE GRACE

IF WE UNDERSTAND THE SIN IN OUR HEARTS

The heart is deceitful above all things, and desperately wicked: who can know it? — *Jeremiah 17:9*

AND WHO DO YOU SAY HE IS?

He saith unto them, But whom say ye that I am? And Simon Peter answered and said,
Thou art the Christ, the Son of the living God. —Matthew 16:15-16

FRIENDS DON'T LET FRIENDS

DIE WITHOUT JESUS

Ointment and perfume rejoice the heart: so doth the sweetness of a man's friend by hearty counsel. —Proverbs 27:9

IF GOD SEEMS FAR AWAY

GUESS WHO MOVED?

Let your conversation be without covetousness; and be content with such things as ye have: for he hath said, I will never leave thee, nor forsake thee. — *Hebrews 13:5*

IN THE DARK?

FOLLOW THE SON

But all things that are reproved are made manifest by the light:for whatsoever doth make manifest is light. Wherefore he saith, Awake thou that sleepest, and arise from the dead, and Christ shall give thee light. —Ephesians 5:13-14

TOGETHER IN CHRIST

But God, who is rich in mercy, for his great love wherewith he loved us, Even when we were dead in sins, hath quickened us together with Christ, (by grace ye are saved;) And hath raised us up together, and made us sit together in heavenly places in Christ Jesus. —Ephesians 2:4-6

CHRISTIANS ARE NOT

PERFECT AND INNOCENT

BUT GUILTY AND FORGIVEN

To open their eyes, and to turn them from darkness to light, and from the power of Satan unto God, that they may receive forgiveness of sins, and inheritance among them which are sanctified by faith that is in me. —Acts 26:18

GOING THE WRONG WAY?
GOD ALLOWS U-TURNS

And saying, The time is fulfilled, and the kingdom of God is at hand: repent ye, and believe the gospel. —Mark 1:15

GREAT THINGS THE LORD HATH DONE

Praise him for his mighty acts: praise him according to his excellent greatness. —*Psalms 150:2*

JESUS DIED

HE AROSE

HE IS COMING AGAIN

Let not your heart be troubled: ye believe in God, believe also in me. In my Father's house are many mansions: if it were not so, I would have told you. I go to prepare a place for you. And if I go and prepare a place for you, I will come again, and receive you unto myself; that where I am, there ye may be also. — John 14:1-3

JESUS IS RISEN AND HE IS LORD

He is not here: for he is risen, as he said.
Come, see the place where the Lord lay. —Matthew 28:6

JESUS SAVIOR

HELPER FRIEND

A man that hath friends must shew himself friendly:
and there is a friend that sticketh closer than a brother. —*Proverbs 18:24*

JESUS SAVIOR SON OF GOD

And the angel answered and said unto her, The Holy Ghost shall come upon thee, and the power of the Highest shall overshadow thee: therefore also that holy thing which shall be born of thee shall be called the Son of God. —Luke 1:35

ONLY ONE MESSIAH HAS AN EMPTY GRAVE

And he saith unto them, Be not affrighted: Ye seek Jesus of Nazareth, which was crucified: he is risen; he is not here: behold the place where they laid him. —Mark 16:6

GOD DOES NOT FORGET THE SINNER

HE FORGETS THE SIN

Whosoever committeth sin transgresseth also the law: for sin is the transgression of the law. And ye know that he was manifested to take away our sins; and in him is no sin. —1 John 3:4-5

WHEN GOD FORGIVES

HE REMOVES THE SIN

AND RESTORES THE SOUL

*If we confess our sins, he is faithful and just to forgive us our sins,
and to cleanse us from all unrighteousness.* —1 John 1:9

JESUS IS LIFE

THE REST IS DETAILS

Jesus saith unto him, I am the way, the truth, and the life: no man cometh unto the Father, but by me. —John 14:6

SALVATION:

FREE TO US

COSTLY TO GOD

But God commendeth his love toward us, in that, while we were yet sinners, Christ died for us. Much more then, being now justified by his blood, we shall be saved from wrath through him. —Romans 5:8-9

THANKS BE TO GOD

FOR HIS UNSPEAKABLE GIFT

Every good gift and every perfect gift is from above, and cometh down from the Father of lights, with whom is no variableness, neither shadow of turning. —James 1:17

THE BEST GIFT

ANYONE CAN RECEIVE

IS JESUS

But after that the kindness and love of God our Saviour toward man appeared, Not by works of righteousness which we have done, but according to his mercy he saved us, by the washing of regeneration, and renewing of the Holy Ghost; Which he shed on us abundantly through Jesus Christ our Saviour. —Titus 3:4-6

PUT FEARS TO REST

BY FAITH IN JESUS

There is no fear in love; but perfect love casteth out fear: because fear hath torment.
He that feareth is not made perfect in love. —*1 John 4:18*

ACCEPT JESUS CHRIST
OR PREPARE TO TAKE THE HEAT

So shall it be at the end of the world: the angels shall come forth, and sever the wicked from among the just, And shall cast them into the furnace of fire: there shall be wailing and gnashing of teeth. —Matthew 13:49-50

DON'T GAMBLE WITH YOUR SOUL

Whereas ye know not what shall be on the morrow. For what is your life?
It is even a vapour, that appeareth for a little time, and then vanisheth away. —James 4:14

WHEN JESUS COMES INTO A LIFE

HE CHANGES EVERYTHING

Therefore if any man be in Christ, he is a new creature: old things are passed away; behold, all things are become new. —2 Corinthians 5:17

MUST WE DIE TO LIVE?

Verily, verily, I say unto you, Except a corn of wheat fall into the ground and die, it abideth alone: but if it die, it bringeth forth much fruit. —John 12:24

CHRIST TAKES US AS WE ARE AND MAKES US WHAT WE OUGHT TO BE

Being confident of this very thing, that he which hath begun a good work in you will perform it until the day of Jesus Christ. —Philippians 1:6

WHAT CAN WE EXPECT FROM HEAVEN?

And the building of the wall of it was of jasper: and the city was pure gold, like unto clear glass. And the foundations of the wall of the city were garnished with all manner of precious stones. —Revelation 21:18-19

ALIVE IS BETTER

JESUS LIVES

And it came to pass, as they were much perplexed thereabout, behold, two men stood by them in shining garments: And as they were afraid, and bowed down their faces to the earth, they said unto them, Why seek ye the living among the dead? He is not here, but is risen. —Luke 24:4-6

CHRIST BELIEVED

HIS SALVATION RECEIVED

That if thou shalt confess with thy mouth the Lord Jesus, and shalt believe in thine heart that God hath raised him from the dead, thou shalt be saved. —Romans 10:9

NO JESUS — NO PEACE

KNOW JESUS — KNOW PEACE

*Grace be with you, mercy, and peace, from God the Father,
and from the Lord Jesus Christ, the Son of the Father, in truth and love.* —2 John 3

DO NOT WAIT FOR THE HEARSE

TO TAKE YOU TO CHURCH

From that time Jesus began to preach, and to say,
Repent: for the kingdom of heaven is at hand. —Matthew 4:17

HE THAT IS BORN ONCE WILL DIE TWICE

HE THAT IS BORN TWICE WILL DIE ONCE

Jesus answered, Verily, verily, I say unto thee, Except a man be born of water and of the Spirit, he cannot enter into the kingdom of God. That which is born of the flesh is flesh; and that which is born of the Spirit is spirit. —John 3:3,6

GOD DOESN'T WANT ABILITY

JUST AVAILABILITY

And Jesus said unto him, No man, having put his hand to the plough, and looking back, is fit for the kingdom of God. —Luke 9:62

SALVATION IS RECEIVED

NOT ACHIEVED

For by grace are ye saved through faith; and that not of yourselves: it is the gift of God: Not of works, lest any man should boast. —Ephesians 2:8-9

IT'S NOT WHAT YOU HAVE IN YOUR LIFE

IT'S WHO YOU HAVE IN YOUR LIFE

But these are written, that ye might believe that Jesus is the Christ, the Son of God; and that believing ye might have life through his name. —John 20:31

DON'T LET A DARK PAST

CLOUD A BRIGHT FUTURE

TODAY IS THE FIRST DAY

OF THE REST OF YOUR LIFE

Therefore we are buried with him by baptism into death: that like as Christ was raised up from the dead by the glory of the Father, even so we also should walk in newness of life. —Romans 6:4

A BIBLE THAT IS FALLING APART

USUALLY REVEALS A LIFE THAT ISN'T

Blessed is the man that walketh not in the counsel of the ungodly, nor standeth in the way of sinners, nor sitteth in the seat of the scornful. But his delight is in the law of the LORD; and in his law doth he meditate day and night. — *Psalms 1:1-2*

WHEN TROUBLE GROWS

YOUR CHARACTER SHOWS

*And not only so, but we glory in tribulations also; knowing that tribulation worketh patience;
And patience, experience; and experience, hope. —Romans 5:3-4*

LOVE DOES NOT DOMINATE

IT CULTIVATES

*And above all things have fervent charity among yourselves:
for charity shall cover the multitude of sins.* —1 Peter 4:8

I WILL GO ANYWHERE GOD CALLS ME

AT ANY PRICE

And Jesus said unto him, Foxes have holes, and birds of the air have nests; but the Son of man hath not where to lay his head. —Luke 9:58

LOVE ONE ANOTHER

And now I beseech thee, lady, not as though I wrote a new commandment unto thee, but that which we had from the beginning, that we love one another. —2 John 5

BRUSH YOUR MIND WITH THE WORD OF GOD

IT PREVENTS TRUTH DECAY

Husbands, love your wives, even as Christ also loved the church, and gave himself for it; That he might sanctify and cleanse it with the washing of water by the word. —Ephesians 5:25-26

GOSSIP THE GOSPEL

And he said unto them, Go ye into all the world, and preach the gospel to every creature. —Mark 16:15

LOST TIME IS NEVER FOUND

*See then that ye walk circumspectly, not as fools, but as wise,
Redeeming the time, because the days are evil.* —Ephesians 5:15-16

CAN'T SLEEP? DON'T COUNT SHEEP

TALK WITH THE SHEPHERD

I am the good shepherd, and know my sheep, and am known of mine. —John 10:14

JESUS IS THE SHEPHERD

I am the good shepherd: the good shepherd giveth his life for the sheep. —*John 10:11*

TO LOVE GOD IS TO OBEY GOD

Jesus answered and said unto him, If a man love me, he will keep my words: and my Father will love him, and we will come unto him, and make our abode with him. —John 14:23

PREPARE YOUR HEART

FOR CHRIST'S RETURN

Return unto me, and I will return unto you, saith the LORD of hosts. —Malachi 3:7

DROUGHT GOT YOU DOWN?

LIVING WATER HERE

In the last day, that great day of the feast, Jesus stood and cried, saying, If any man thirst, let him come unto me, and drink. He that believeth on me, as the scripture hath said, out of his belly shall flow rivers of living water. —John 7:37-38

JESUS

OUR ROCK AND SHELTER IN THE STORM

And did all drink the same spiritual drink: for they drank of that spiritual Rock that followed them: and that Rock was Christ. —1 Corinthians 10:4

THE DEEP PEACE OF GOD

And the peace of God, which passeth all understanding,
shall keep your hearts and minds through Christ Jesus. —Philippians 4:7

TRUTH IS ALWAYS

THE STRONGEST ARGUMENT

Then said Jesus to those Jews which believed on him, If ye continue in my word,
then are ye my disciples indeed; And ye shall know the truth,
and the truth shall make you free. —John 8:31-32

HE STILL SPEAKS TO

THOSE WHO LISTEN

And the LORD came, and stood, and called as at other times, Samuel, Samuel. Then Samuel answered, Speak; for thy servant heareth. —1 Samuel 3:10

GOD MEETS OUR NEEDS

IN UNEXPECTED WAYS

Now unto him that is able to do exceeding abundantly above all that we ask or think, according to the power that worketh in us. —*Ephesians 3:20*

THE LORD IS MY HELPER

I WILL NOT BE AFRAID

*So that we may boldly say, The Lord is my helper,
and I will not fear what man shall do unto me. —Hebrews 13:6*

NOT ABLE? JESUS IS!

I can do all things through Christ which strengtheneth me. — *Philippians 4:13*

GLORY TO GOD IN THE HIGHEST HEAVEN

And suddenly there was with the angel a multitude of the heavenly host praising God, and saying, Glory to God in the highest, and on earth peace, good will toward men. —Luke 2:13-14

IF YOU FIND IT HARD TO STAND FOR JESUS

TRY KNEELING FIRST

O come, let us worship and bow down:
let us kneel before the LORD our maker. — *Psalms 95:6*

PRAYER IS AN OPEN LINE TO HEAVEN

For there is one God, and one mediator between God and men, the man Christ Jesus; Who gave himself a ransom for all, to be testified in due time. —1 Timothy 2:5-6

IF WE ARE TOO BUSY TO PRAY

WE ARE TOO BUSY

Rejoice evermore. Pray without ceasing. In every thing give thanks: for this is the will of God in Christ Jesus concerning you. —1 Thessalonians 5:16-18

THE BEST WAY TO REMEMBER PEOPLE

IS IN PRAYER

Confess your faults one to another, and pray one for another, that ye may be healed. The effectual fervent prayer of a righteous man availeth much. — James 5:16

THANKFULNESS IS THE SOIL

THAT JOY THRIVES IN

Enter into his gates with thanksgiving, and into his courts with praise: be thankful unto him, and bless his name. —Psalms 100:4

GOD NEVER TIRES OF HEARING US IN PRAYER

But thou, when thou prayest, enter into thy closet, and when thou hast shut thy door, pray to thy Father which is in secret; and thy Father which seeth in secret shall reward thee openly. —*Matthew 6:6*

PRAYER OFTEN BEGINS WITH

A CONFESSION OF SIN

And I prayed unto the LORD my God, and made my confession, and said, O Lord, the great and dreadful God, keeping the covenant and mercy to them that love him, and to them that keep his commandments —Daniel 9:4

LET EVERYTHING ALIVE PRAISE THE LORD

Praise ye the LORD. Praise ye the LORD from the heavens: praise him in the heights. Praise him, all his angels: praise ye him, all his hosts. Praise him, sun and moon: praise him, all ye stars of light. Praise him, ye heavens of heavens, and ye waters that be above the heavens. —*Psalms 148:1-4*

GREAT PRAISE

OFTEN GROWS OUT OF

GREAT PAIN

In God I will praise his word, in God I have put my trust;
I will not fear what flesh can do unto me. —*Psalms 56:4*

THE BEST THINGS IN LIFE

ARE NOT THINGS

Through wisdon is an house builded; and by understanding it is established; And by knowledge shall the chambers be filled with all precious and pleasant riches. —Proberbs 24:3-4

A WORD OF LOVE CAN MAKE

A WORLD OF DIFFERENCE

*A wholesome tongue is a tree of life:
but perverseness therein is a breach in the spirit.* — *Proverbs 15:4*

CHILDREN

AN HERITAGE OF THE LORD

Lo, children are an heritage of the LORD: and the fruit of the womb is his reward.
As arrows are in the hand of a mighty man; so are children of the youth.
Happy is the man that hath his quiver full of them: they shall not be ashamed,
but they shall speak with the enemies in the gate. —*Psalms 127:3-4*

BLESSED IS HE

WHO TRUSTS IN THE LORD

But it is good for me to draw near to God:
I have put my trust in the Lord GOD,
that I may declare all thy works. —*Psalms 73:28*

COUNT YOUR BLESSINGS

NOT YOUR TROUBLES

Blessed be the God and Father of our Lord Jesus Christ,
who hath blessed us with all spiritual blessings in heavenly places in Christ. —Ephesians 1:3

THE LORD BLESSES HIS PEOPLE WITH PEACE

Peace I leave with you, my peace I give unto you: not as the world giveth, give I unto you. Let not your heart be troubled, neither let it be afraid. —John 14:27

DISCIPLINE

IS DOING SOMETHING YOU DISLIKE

TO CREATE SOMETHING YOU LOVE

And beside this, giving all diligence, add to your faith virtue; and to virtue knowledge;
And to knowledge temperance; and to temperance patience; and to patience godliness;
And to godliness brotherly kindness; and to brotherly kindness charity. —2 Peter 1:5-7

CONTENTMENT

ENJOYING THE SCENERY ON A DETOUR

*Not that I speak in respect of want: for I have learned,
in whatsoever state I am, therewith to be content.* —*Philippians 4:11*

AT THE END OF YOUR ROPE?

LOOK UP

Looking unto Jesus the author and finisher of our faith;
who for the joy that was set before him endured the cross, despising the shame,
and is set down at the right hand of the throne of God. —Hebrews 12:2

TROUBLE LOOKS BACK

WORRY LOOKS AHEAD

FAITH LOOKS UP

But without faith it is impossible to please him: for he that cometh to God must believe that he is, and that he is a rewarder of them that diligently seek him. —Hebrews 11:6

HAVE PATIENCE

FOR IN TIME THE GRASS BECOMES MILK

Wait on the LORD: be of good courage, and he shall strengthen thine heart: wait, I say, on the LORD. — *Psalms 27:14*

A DIAMOND IS A PIECE OF COAL

THAT STUCK TO THE JOB

And he shall sit as a refiner and purifier of silver: and he shall purify the sons of Levi, and purge them as gold and silver, that they may offer unto the LORD an offering in righteousness. —Malachi 3:3

HAPPINESS IS AN INSIDE JOB

Trust in the LORD, and do good; so shalt thou dwell in the land, and verily thou shalt be fed. Delight thyself also in the LORD; and he shall give thee the desires of thine heart. — Psalms 37:3-4

EVERY CHILD SHOULD BE

WELL FED AND WELL LED

Train up a child in the way he should go:
and when he is old, he will not depart from it. —*Proverbs 22:6*

IT IS NOT WHERE WE SERVE

IT'S WHETHER WE SERVE THAT'S IMPORTANT

And if it seem evil unto you to serve the LORD, choose you this day whom ye will serve;
whether the gods which your fathers served that were on the other side of the flood,
or the gods of the Amorites, in whose land ye dwell: but as for me and my house,
we will serve the LORD. —Joshua 24:15

KINDNESS IS THE HARDEST THING

TO GIVE AWAY

IT ALWAYS COMES BACK

Give, and it shall be given unto you; good measure, pressed down, and shaken together, and running over, shall men give into your bosom. For with the same measure that ye mete withal it shall be measured to you again. —Luke 6:38

GOOD AND HATE

CANNOT DWELL IN THE SAME HEART

Be ye not unequally yoked together with unbelievers: for what fellowship hath righteousness with unrighteousness? and what communion hath light with darkness? And what concord hath Christ with Belial? or what part hath he that believeth with an infidel? —2 Corinthians 6:14-15

BUILDING BOYS IS BETTER

THAN MENDING MEN

A wise son maketh a glad father: but a foolish man despiseth his mother. —*Proverbs 15:20*

FRIENDSHIP MULTIPLIES YOUR JOYS

AND DIVIDES YOUR SORROWS

Iron sharpeneth iron; so a man sharpeneth the countenance of his friend. —*Proverbs 27:17*

PAY ATTENTION TO THE IMPULSE TO CARE

But a certain Samaritan, as he journeyed, came where he was: and when he saw him, he had compassion on him, And went to him, and bound up his wounds, pouring in oil and wine, and set him on his own beast, and brought him to an inn, and took care of him. —Luke 10:33-34

PRAISE LOUDLY

BLAME SOFTLY

A soft answer turneth away wrath: but grievous words stir up anger. The tongue of the wise useth knowledge aright: but the mouth of fools poureth out foolishness. —Proverbs 15:1-2

THE EASIEST THING TO CONFESS IS

MY NEIGHBOR'S SIN

Be not a witness against thy neighbour without cause;
and deceive not with thy lips. — *Proverbs 24:28*

TO SEE YOURSELF AS YOU REALLY ARE

LOOK INTO THE MIRROR OF GOD'S WORD

For now we see through a glass, darkly; but then face to face: now I know in part; but then shall I know even as also I am known. —1 Corinthians 13:12

TODAY'S DECISIONS

ARE TOMORROW'S REALITIES

Multitudes, multitudes in the valley of decision:
for the day of the LORD is near in the valley of decision. — Joel 3:14

TRY GOING THE SECOND MILE

THERE'S NO TRAFFIC JAM THERE

And whosoever shall compel thee to go a mile, go with him twain. —*Matthew 5:41*

TRYING TIMES ARE NO TIME TO STOP TRYING

Beloved, think it not strange concerning the fiery trial which is to try you,
as though some strange thing happened unto you. —1 Peter 4:12

YOUR ACTIONS ARE LIVING PROOF

OF WHAT YOU BELIEVE ABOUT GOD

Abide in me, and I in you. As the branch cannot bear fruit of itself, except it abide in the vine;
no more can ye, except ye abide in me. I am the vine, ye are the branches:
He that abideth in me, and I in him, the same bringeth forth much fruit:
for without me ye can do nothing. — John 15:4-5

UNTIL YOU SPREAD YOUR WINGS

YOU HAVE NO IDEA HOW FAR YOU CAN FLY

*But they that wait upon the LORD shall renew their strength;
they shall mount up with wings as eagles; they shall run, and not be weary;
and they shall walk, and not faint.* —*Isaiah 40:31*

LAUGHTER CURES MORE ILLS THAN PILLS

A merry heart doeth good like a medicine: but a broken spirit drieth the bones. — *Proverbs 17:22*

BE RICH IN DEEDS

FOR GOD WANTS YOU TO BE GENEROUS

IN MEETING OTHERS' NEEDS

And whatsoever ye do in word or deed, do all in the name of the Lord Jesus, giving thanks to God and the Father by him. —Colossians 3:17

BETTER TO RISE TO THE OCCASION

THAN TO HIT THE CEILING

He that is slow to anger is better than the mighty;
and he that ruleth his spirit than he that taketh a city. —*Proverbs 16:32*

FORGET YOUR TROUBLES

BY HELPING OTHERS

Therefore if thine enemy hunger, feed him; if he thirst, give him drink: for in so doing thou shalt heap coals of fire on his head. —Romans 12:20

GIVE GOD WHAT IS RIGHT

NOT WHAT IS LEFT

Honour the LORD with thy substance, and with the firstfruits of all thine increase: So shall thy barns be filled with plenty, and thy presses shall burst out with new wine. — Proverbs 3:9-10

MORE PEOPLE GET RUN DOWN BY GOSSIP

THAN BY CARS

Let the words of my mouth, and the meditation of my heart, be acceptable in thy sight, O LORD, my strength, and my redeemer. —*Psalms 19:14*

IF GOD IS YOUR COPILOT

CHANGE SEATS

Trust in the LORD with all thine heart; and lean not unto thine own understanding. In all thy ways acknowledge him, and he shall direct thy paths. — Proverbs 3:5-6

GODLY FATHERS

REFLECT THE LOVE OF OUR HEAVENLY FATHER

If ye then, being evil, know how to give good gifts unto your children: how much more shall your heavenly Father give the Holy Spirit to them that ask him? — *Luke 11:13*

PEOPLE SELDOM GET DIZZY

DOING GOOD TURNS

My little children, let us not love in word, neither in tongue; but in deed and in truth. —1 John 3:18

COME AND GROW WITH US

Behold, how good and how pleasant it is for brethren to dwell together in unity! — *Psalms 133:1*

COME JUST AS YOU ARE

TO WORSHIP, COME

Come unto me, all ye that labour and are heavy laden, and I will give you rest. —*Matthew 11:28*

COME IN FOR A FAITH LIFT

Flee also youthful lusts: but follow righteousness, faith, charity, peace, with them that call on the Lord out of a pure heart. —2 Timothy 2:22

SIGN BROKEN

MESSAGE INSIDE

This then is the message which we have heard of him, and declare unto you, that God is light, and in him is no darkness at all. —1 John 1:5

OPEN ON SUNDAY

VISITORS EXPECTED

My soul, wait thou only upon God; for my expectation is from him. —*Psalms 62:5*

WE'VE BEEN UNDER THE SAME MANAGEMENT FOR 2000 YEARS

That thou art Peter, and upon this rock I will build my church; and the gates of hell shall not prevail against it. —*Matthew 16:18*

LOVE IS MUSIC IN SEARCH OF WORDS

Praise him with the sound of the trumpet: praise him with the psaltery and harp. Praise him with the timbrel and dance: praise him with stringed instruments and organs. Praise him upon the loud cymbals: praise him upon the high sounding cymbals. Let every thing that hath breath praise the LORD. Praise ye the LORD. —*Psalms 150:3-6*

TO SPEAK KINDLY

DOES NOT HURT THE TONGUE

There is that speaketh like the piercings of a sword: but the tongue of the wise is health. —*Proverb 12:18*

LISTENING

IS THE PUREST FORM OF SELF-DENIAL

Wherefore, my beloved brethren, let every man be swift to hear, slow to speak, slow to wrath: For the wrath of man worketh not the righteousness of God. — James 1:19-20

NEVER USE A GALLON OF WORDS

TO EXPRESS A SPOONFUL OF THOUGHTS

If any man among you seem to be religious, and bridleth not his tongue, but deceiveth his own heart, this man's religion is vain. — James 1:26

NOTHING RUINS THE TRUTH

LIKE STRETCHING IT

By mercy and truth iniquity is purged:
and by the fear of the LORD men depart from evil. — Proverbs 16:6

THIS EASTER DISCOVER

HOPE FOR THE FUTURE

But I will hope continually, and will yet praise thee more and more. — *Psalms 71:14*

WANT THE GOOD LIFE?

READ THE OWNER'S MANUAL

Let us hear the conclusion of the whole matter: Fear God, and keep his commandments: for this is the whole duty of man. For God shall bring every work into judgment, with every secret thing, whether it be good, or whether it be evil. —Ecclesiastes 12:13

DEAR READER,

If you would like to contribute a church sign quote for our upcoming American Signs of Faith—Church Signs in the Land of the Free, please send it to us at one of the following addresses:

Exponential Publications, PO Box 300
Intercourse, PA 17534-0300

Email: churchsigns@frontiernet.net

Please include the City and State of where the quote is from. We will add you to our mailing list and will notify you when those editions will be released. From one of Lancaster County's Old Order English Families.

About the Author

PETE BECKARY RELOCATED TO LANCASTER COUNTY WITH HIS FAMILY IN 1998.
HE APPRECIATES AND ENJOYS THE VALUES AND CULTURE OF THE AREA.
HE IS SELF-EMPLOYED DOING ACCOUNTING AND COMPUTER CONSULTING.

About the Photographer

DR. ROBERT LEAHY IS A PROMINENT PHOTOGRAPHER OF THE AMISH
AND MENNONITE COMMUNITIES OF LANCASTER COUNTY, BEST KNOWN
FOR DEPICTING THE SIMPLICITY OF THEIR EVERYDAY LIVES.